the Selah
SONGBOOK
the

the Selah SONGBOOK

Includes all of the songs from "PRESS ON"
Also included from "BE STILL MY SOUL"

THE BLOOD WILL NEVER LOSE ITS POWER • HIS EYE IS ON THE SPARROW • IT IS WELL WITH MY SOUL • ONE THING I KNOW

Transcribed by
Bryan Cullifer and Bryce Inman

Edited by
Bryce Inman

WORD MUSIC®

"It can be compared to the man who sails from England looking for the New World. When he finally sees

land he's amazed at the beauty of it and stakes his claim, only to find out that it's actually still England. He had just never seen the country before in that light. That's how we feel about the great hymns and spirituals. They're such a musical and theological treasure, and yet they're too often taken for granted. We're trying to reinterpret those songs in a new light."

—Nicol Smith

Selah

It certainly wasn't what they expected when they took a week off from their other pursuits to record a few songs for the benefit of their family and friends—sales of 100,000 units, a Dove Award for Inspirational Album of the Year, appearances on shows like the 700 Club. No, when stellar pianist Allan Hall along with gifted sibling vocalists Todd and Nicol Smith produced their simple but stirring collection of hymns and spirituals entitled *Be Still My Soul*, it was only intended to be a gift of encouragement for those who had long supported and encouraged them. True, they had played a few local gigs together under the name Selah, but their trio venture was just a fun sideline they dabbled in together.

Emphasis on *was*.

After the front office at Curb Records got a copy of *Be Still My Soul*, signed the group and released the project as it was, things slowly began to shift. At the time, Nicol was still concentrating on her R&B styled solo recording for Curb. Allan and Todd were pursuing their own separate musical ventures as well. So, there weren't any great expectations for the Selah record. The project was just tossed into the retail pond where it made a few ripples that somehow, and inexplicably, seemed to keep spreading.

And spreading.

The reality was that people who were discovering *Be Still My Soul* couldn't seem to keep it to themselves. Selah's sparse and soulful renditions of familiar, half-remembered songs of theologically rich praise and heartfelt worship were striking a chord with a wide cross-section of listeners spanning a broad age range. As one teenage fan explained, "I bought one for myself, one for my mother, and one for my grandmother!" That kind of spontaneous, grassroots, word-of-mouth exposure eventually reached a critical mass, lifting Selah to a level of industry acclaim and commercial success that they had never envisioned. "It even took the record company by surprise," Todd admits.

Their follow-up Curb release, *Press On*, offers the same unique chemistry as *Be Still My Soul*, albeit with a bit more octane. Given a recording budget and a free reign artistically, Selah and Jason Kyle produced a project that flows naturally from—while extending the scope of—their earlier effort.

"Older people are glad to see that the hymns that have meant so much to them aren't just going to die out," Nicol adds. "We've had 70-year-old people come up to us after a concert and say, 'My grandmother used to sing me that song when I was a kid.' These songs form a unique and special bridge to the past for a lot of people, and at the same time they can be brand new to a younger generation."

"I think we'll always love working with the simple melodies of the hymns," Allan says. "Hymns are so well crafted to begin with, so well written lyrically. Their musical simplicity allows the heart and the emotional honesty to come through. That's why they so effectively communicate joy and hope and comfort and encouragement to people."

One of the most obviously unique elements in Selah's music is directly attributable to Todd and Nicol's own African roots. Growing up as part of a missionary family stationed in the Congo, they not only learned to speak the local Kituba dialect, but they absorbed the indigenous musical influences as well. In addition to the blatant rhythms and intricate vocal layerings of the straightforward Congolese praise song "Yesu Azali Awa" (Jesus is here with us), Todd and Nicol's African heritage asserts itself more sublimely elsewhere on *Press On*.

"African music is just a part of us," Todd explains. "It's what we grew up with. It's in our blood. We've been singing it since we were seven years old. When we perform the African songs live, audiences really respond to it."

Seeking a different sort of response, Selah has recently partnered with Todd and Nicol's parents in an effort to raise $500,000 for a hospital facility in the region of the Congo where they still live and minister.

"There's so much need there," Todd says, "and people die needlessly from so many treatable illnesses. We want to help these people live better lives, physically as well as spiritually. We want them to hear the Gospel, but we want them to experience God's mercy in action too. We're inviting all of our friends to be a part of this lifesaving hospital project with us."

"It really is our hope," Todd adds in summation, "that people will see God in a real way through our music. The bottom line is that we want them to see and know His faithfulness, His forgiveness, and His love."

Contents

Oh, Draw Me, Lord

**Words and Music by
DAVID BARONI**
*Arr. Nicol Smith, Todd Smith
and Allan Hall*

Tenderly, with a steady tempo

Oh, draw me, Lord, Oh,

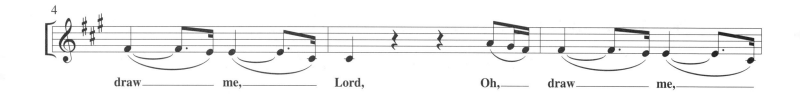

draw me, Lord, Oh, draw me,

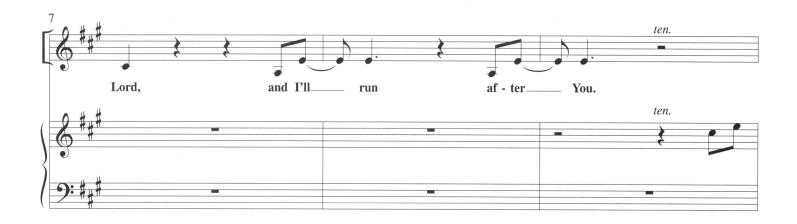

Lord, and I'll run af-ter You.

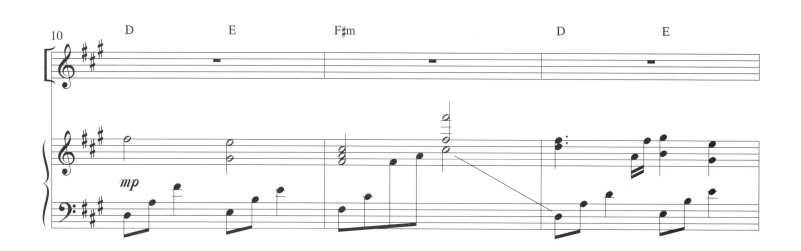

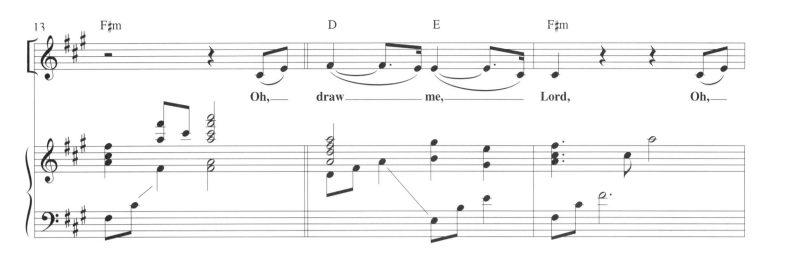

18

There Is a Fountain

Words and Music by
WILLIAM COWPER and
LOWELL MASON

Arr. by Nicol Smith, Todd Smith,
and Allan Hall

Tenderly, with a steady tempo

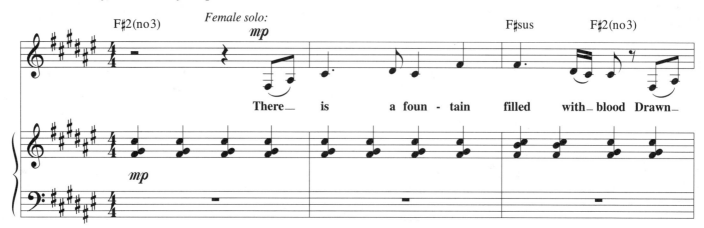

In My Life/
If We Never Meet Again

Gently, with some freedom

"In My Life" - Words and Music by John Lennon and Paul McCartney

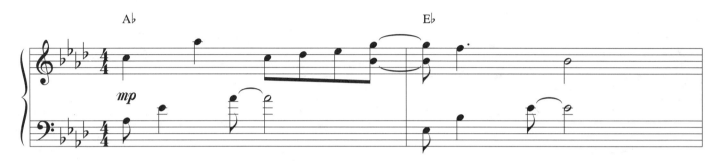

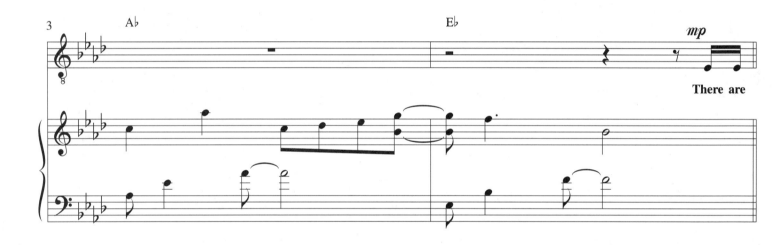

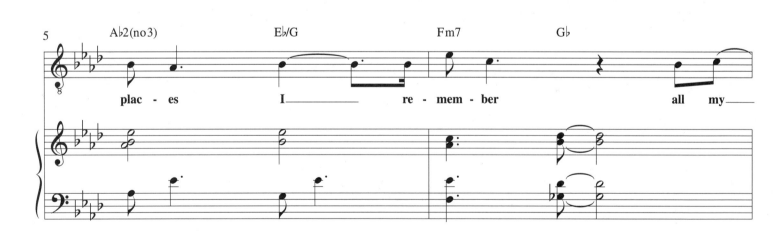

"If We Never Meet Again" - Albert E. Brumley

loved you more.

Soon we'll come to the end of life's

jour-ney, and per-haps we'll nev-er

meet an - y more, 'til we

Hold On

Words and Music by
JESSE DIXON

44

Wonderful, Merciful Savior

Words and Music by
DAWN RODGERS
and ERIC WYSE

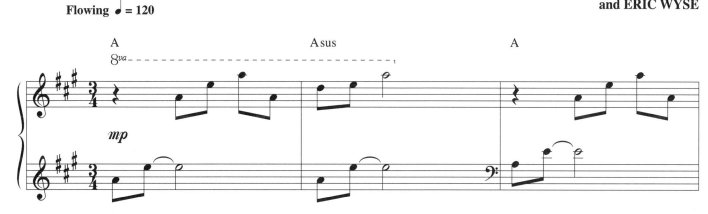

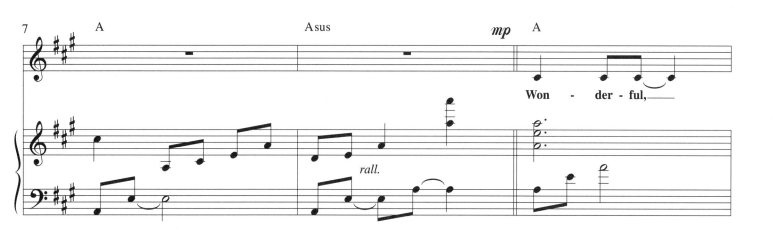

Won - der - ful,____

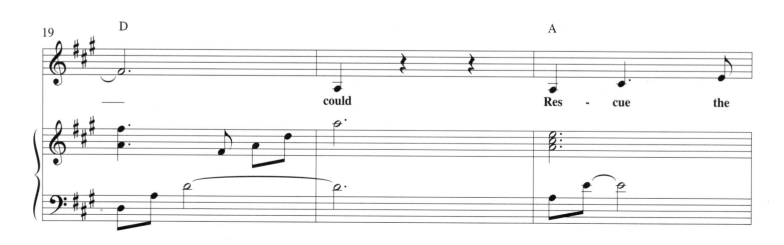

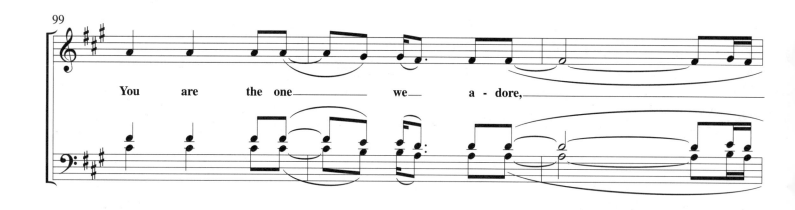

You are the one_____ we__ a - dore,_____

You give the heal - ing__ and

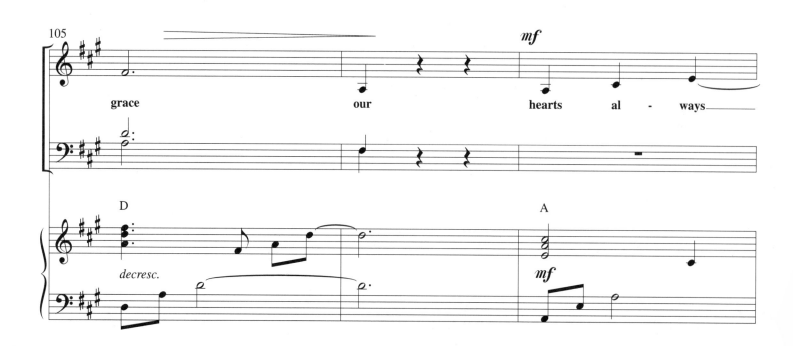

grace our hearts al - ways_____

Were You There?

Traditional Spiritual
Arr. by Russ Taff
and James Hollihan

Freely, with much emotion

57

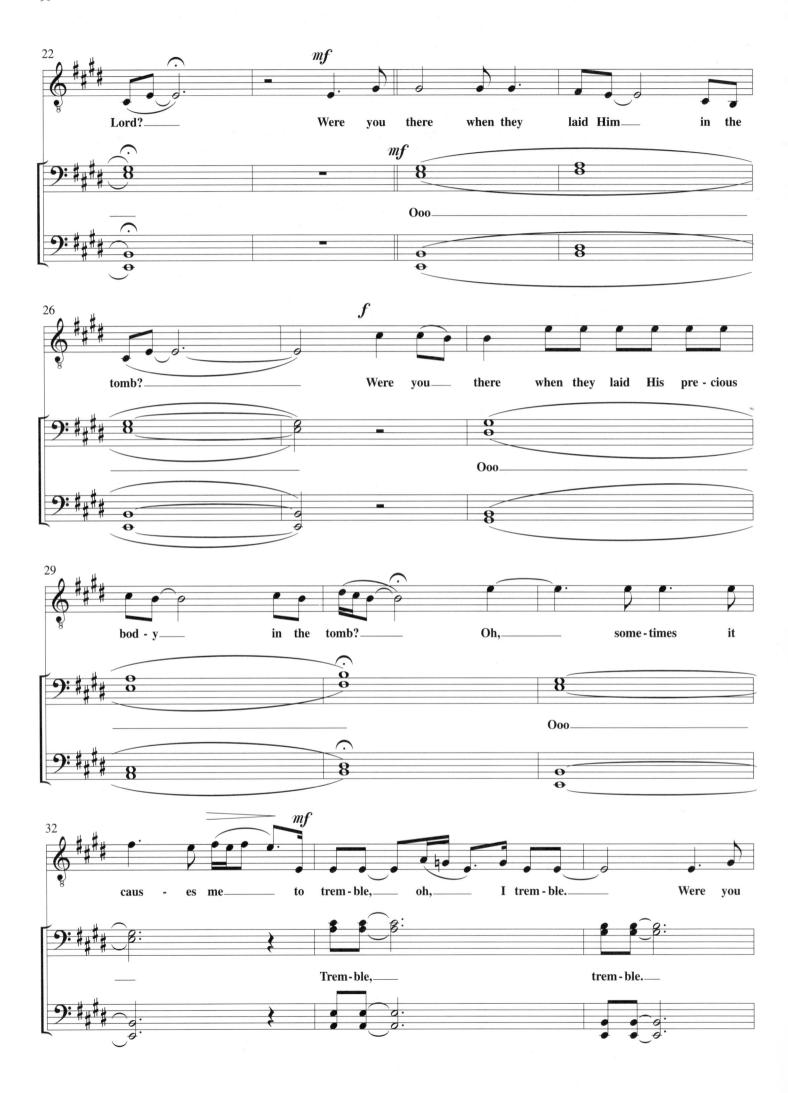

Deep (Way Down)

With a driving beat ♩ = 120

Traditional Spiritual
Arr. by Nicol Smith, Todd Smith,
Allan Hall and Steve Smallman

Yesu Azali Awa
(Jesus Is Here with Us)

Congolese Hymn, author unknown
Translation by Todd Smith and Nicol Smith
Arr. by Nicol Smith, Todd Smith
and Allan Hall

Timeless

Words and Music by
LEVI KREIS

Gently ♩ = 58

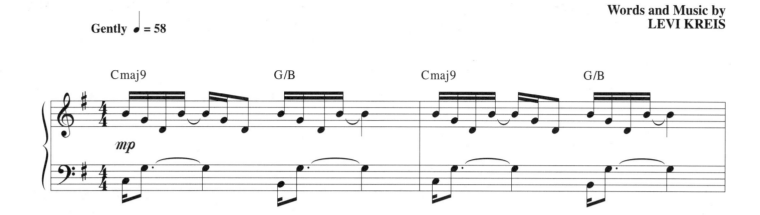

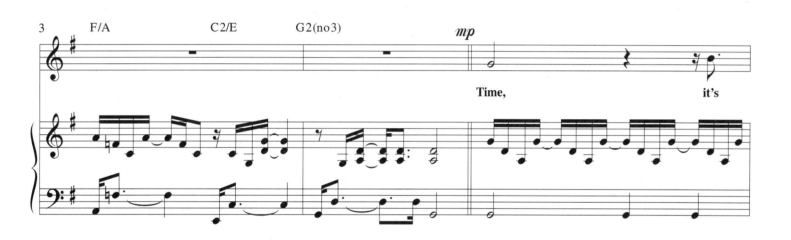

Time, it's

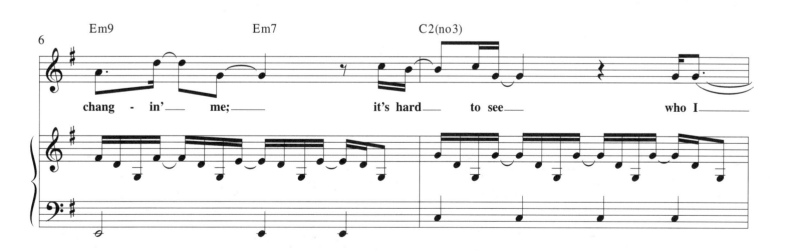

chang - in' me; it's hard to see who I

2nd time to CODA ⊕

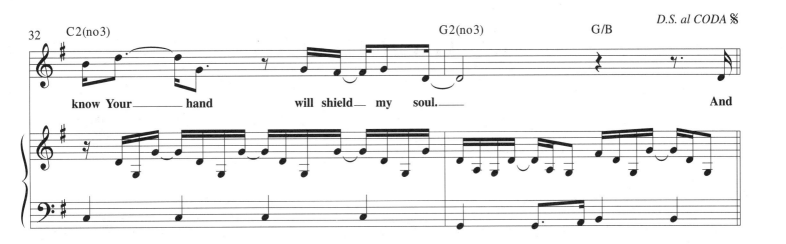

⊕ CODA

How Great Thou Art

Words and Music by
STUART K. HINE

Freely

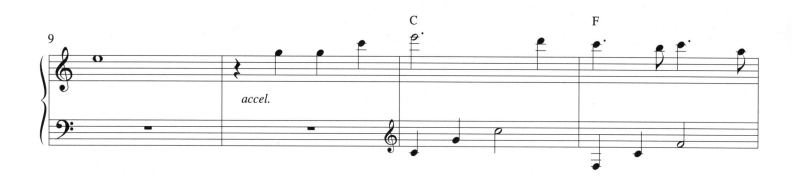

O Lord, my God, when I in awe - some won - der Con - si - der

Amazing Grace

JOHN NEWTON

Traditional American melody
*Arr. by Nicol Smith, Todd Smith
and Allan Hall*

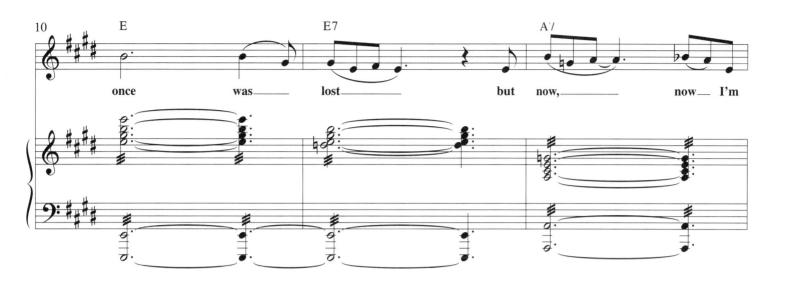

once   was___   lost___   but   now,___   now___ I'm

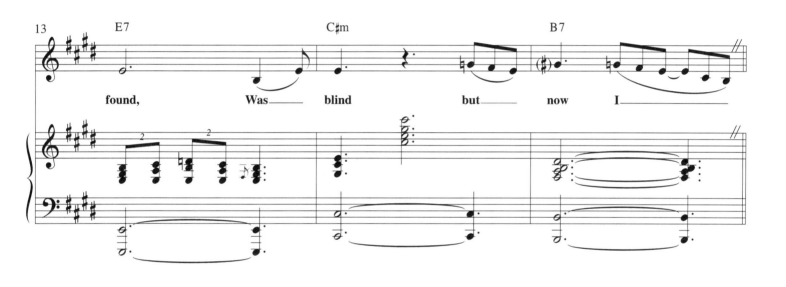

found,   Was___   blind   but___   now   I___

see.___

Press On

Words and Music by
DAN BURGESS

With strength ♩ = 72

Female solo:

When the val - ley — is deep,

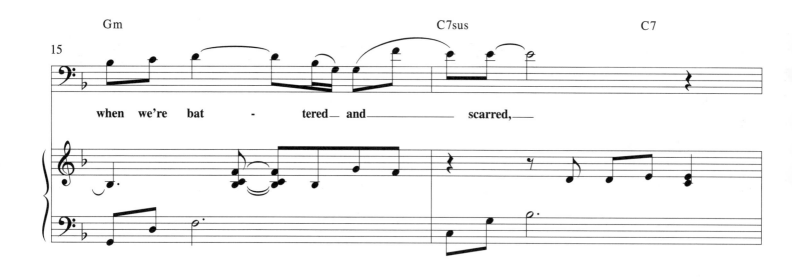

when we're bat - tered— and———— scarred,—

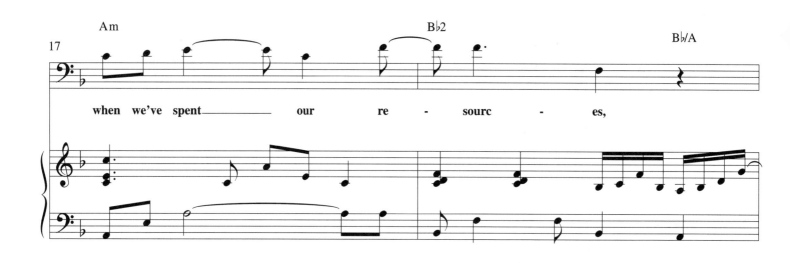

when we've spent———— our re - sourc - es,

when we've giv - en our all,

strength   to press on.

Gm7   C7   F   Am

strength   to press on.

Gm   C7   F

In   Je - sus'

D   D7   G

The Blood Will Never Lose Its Power

Words and Music by
ANDRAÉ CROUCH

Gospel feel ♩. = 84

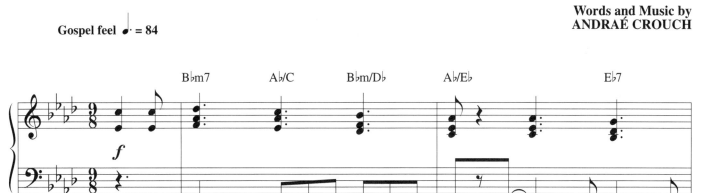

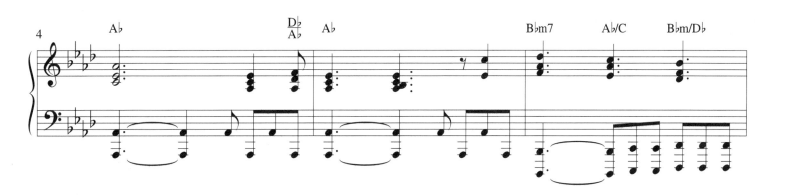

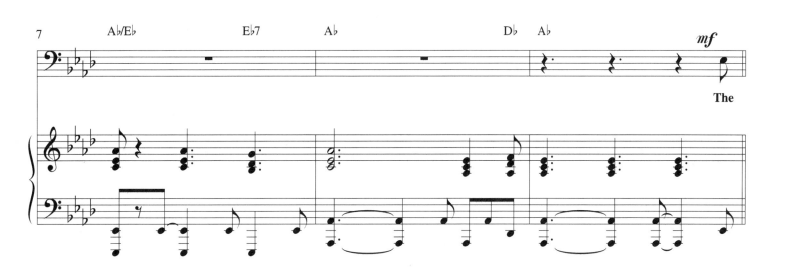

Lyrics:
nev - er lose its pow'r.

It reach - es to the high - est

moun - tain, and it flows to the

His Eye Is on the Sparrow

CIVILLA D. MARTIN

CHARLES H. GABRIEL
*Arr. by Nicol Smith, Todd Smith
and Allan Hall*

It Is Well with My Soul

HORATIO G. SPAFFORD

PHILIP P. BLISS
*Arr. by Nicol Smith, Todd Smith
and Allan Hall*

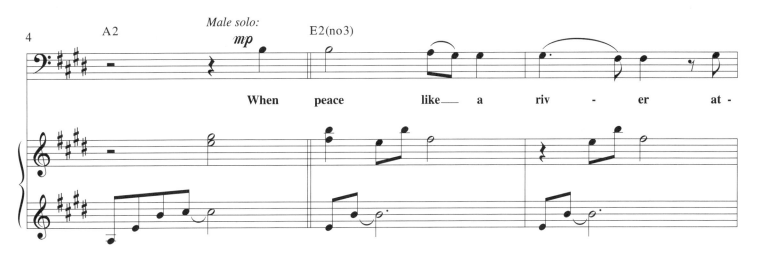

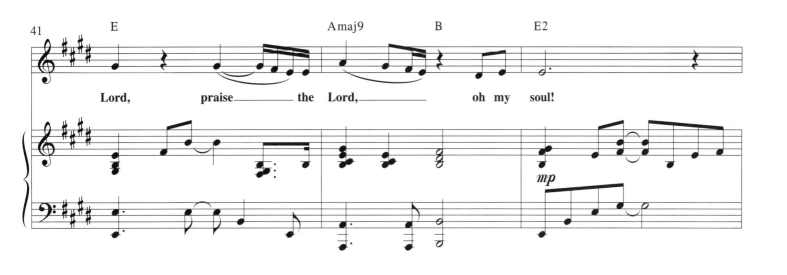

Lord, praise the Lord, oh my soul!

It is well with my

It is well

soul,

It is well, it is

with my soul,

One Thing I Know

Words and Music by
JASON ALAN WHITMORE
and JOEL LINDSAY

Steady four ♩ = 63

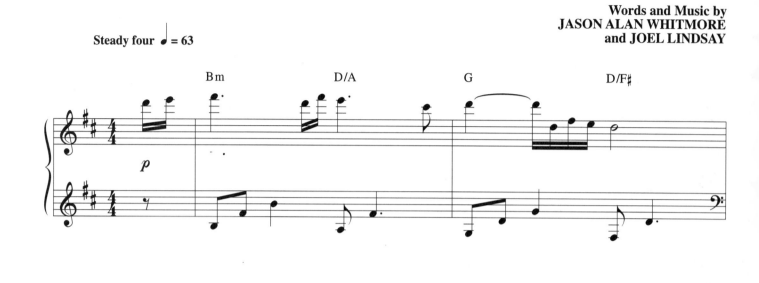

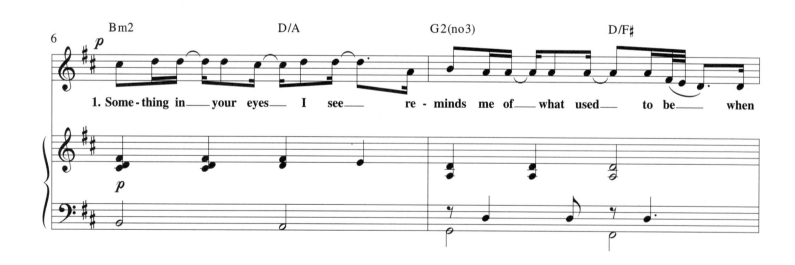

1. Some-thing in your eyes I see re-minds me of what used to be when

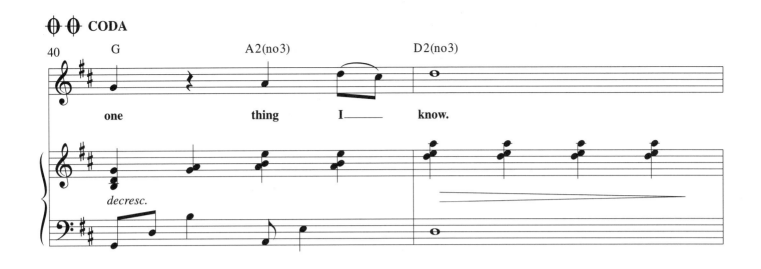

one thing I___ know.

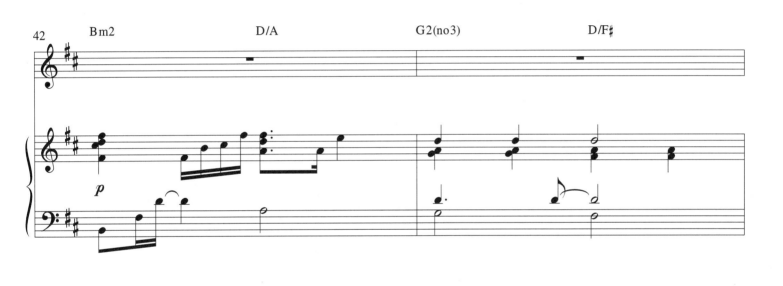